MUSIC FROM AND INSPIRED BY

C000124698

THE PIANIST

A ROMAN POLANSKI FILM

CHESTER MUSIC

LONDON / NEW YORK / PARIS / SYDNEY / COPENHAGEN / BERLIN MADRID / TOKYO

PUBLISHED BY:

CHESTER MUSIC LIMITED
8-9 FRITH STREET, LONDON, W1D 3JB.

EXCLUSIVE DISTRIBUTORS:

MUSIC SALES LIMITED
NEWMARKET ROAD, BURY ST EDMUNDS, SUFFOLK, IP33 3YB, ENGLAND.

MUSIC SALES CORPORATION
257 PARK AVENUE SOUTH, NEW YORK, NY10010, UNITED STATES OF AMERICA.

MUSIC SALES PTY LIMITED
120 ROTHSCHILD AVENUE, ROSEBERY, NSW 2018, AUSTRALIA.

ORDER NO. CH66583
ISBN 1-84449-001-7
THIS BOOK © COPYRIGHT 2003 CHESTER MUSIC.

MUSIC ENGRAVED BY JERRY LANNING AND NOTE-ORIOUS PRODUCTIONS LIMITED.
PRINTED IN THE UNITED KINGDOM.

YOUR GUARANTEE OF QUALITY:
AS PUBLISHERS, WE STRIVE TO PRODUCE EVERY BOOK TO THE HIGHEST COMMERCIAL STANDARDS.
THIS BOOK HAS BEEN FRESHLY ENGRAVED AND AVOIDS AWKWARD PAGE TURNS MAKING PLAYING FROM IT A REAL PLEASURE.
PARTICULAR CARE HAS BEEN GIVEN TO SPECIFYING ACID-FREE, NEUTRAL-SIZED PAPER MADE FROM
PULPS WHICH HAVE NOT BEEN ELEMENTAL CHLORINE BLEACHED.
THE PULP IS FROM FARMED SUSTAINABLE FORESTS AND WAS PRODUCED WITH SPECIAL REGARD FOR THE ENVIRONMENT.
THROUGHOUT, THE PRINTING AND BINDING HAVE BEEN PLANNED TO ENSURE A STURDY,
ATTRACTIVE PUBLICATION WHICH SHOULD GIVE YEARS OF ENJOYMENT.
IF YOUR COPY FAILS TO MEET OUR HIGH STANDARDS, PLEASE INFORM US AND WE WILL GLADLY REPLACE IT.

WWW.MUSICSALES.COM

Nocturne in C-sharp Minor (1830)

Music by Frédéric Chopin
Arranged by Jerry Lanning

Lento con gran espressione   (♩ = 68)

Nocturne in E Minor
Op.72, No.1

Music by Frédéric Chopin
Arranged by Jerry Lanning

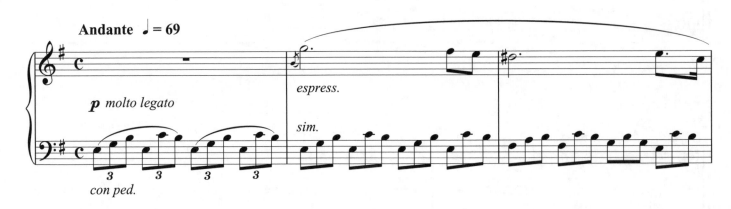

Nocturne in C Minor
Op.48, No.1

Music by Frédéric Chopin
Arranged by Jerry Lanning

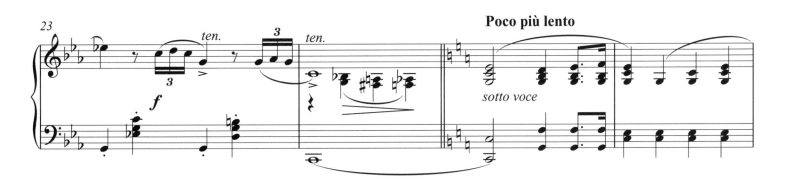

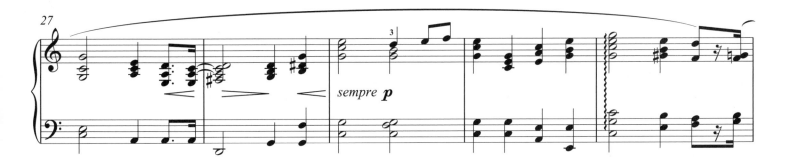

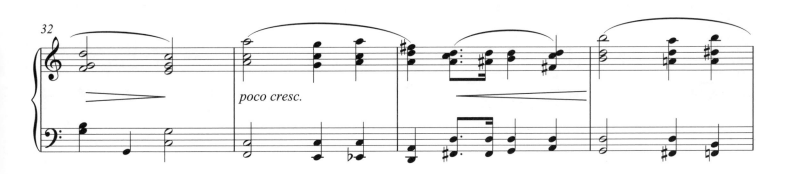

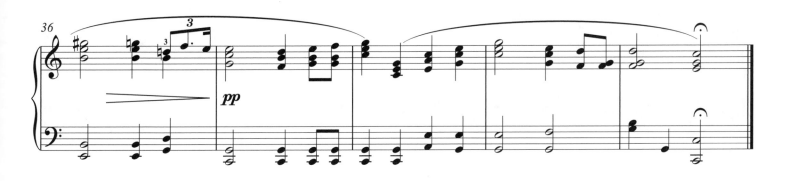

Ballade No.2 in F Major, Op.38

Music by Frédéric Chopin

Andantino ♩. = 72

sotto voce

legato sempre

Ballade No.1 in G Minor, Op.23

Music by Frédéric Chopin
Arranged by Jerry Lanning

Meno mosso ($\quarternote$ = 120)

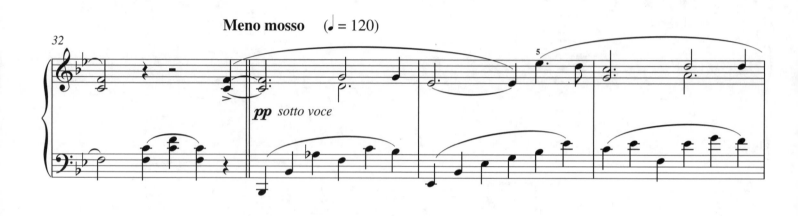

pp *sotto voce*

Waltz No.3 in A Minor
Op.34, No.2

Music by Frédéric Chopin

Poco più mosso

Prélude in E Minor
Op.28, No.4

Music by Frédéric Chopin

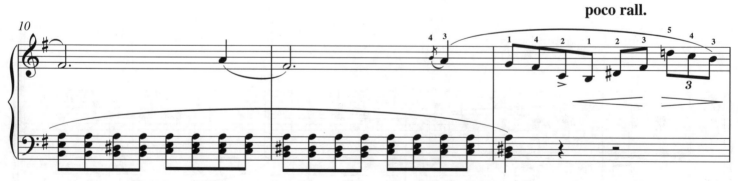

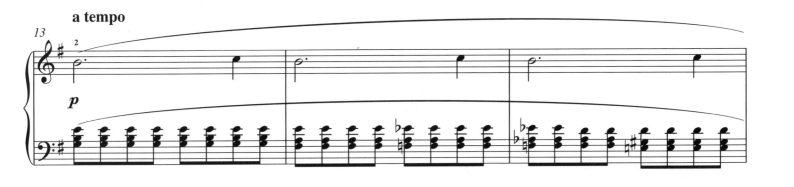

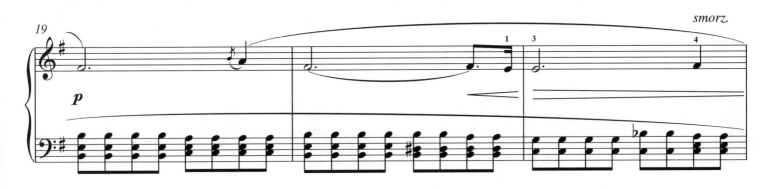

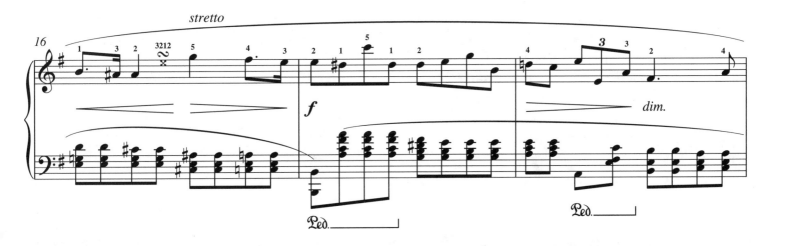

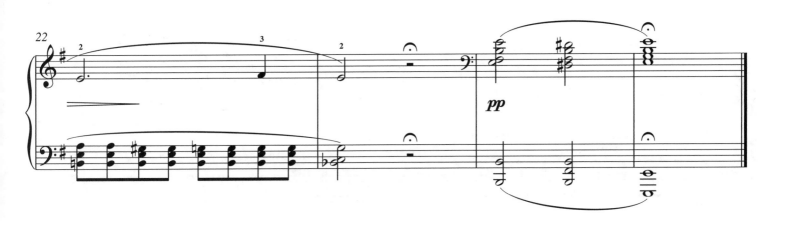

Grande Polonaise brillante in E-flat Major

(preceded by an Andante spianato in G major)

Op.22

Music by Frédéric Chopin
Arranged by Jerry Lanning

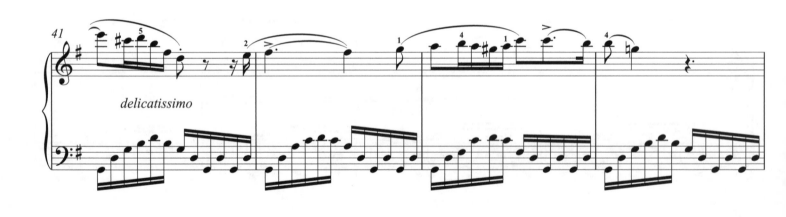

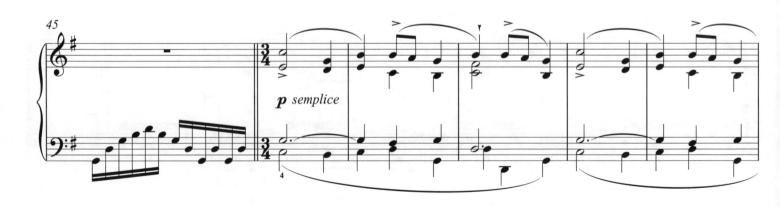

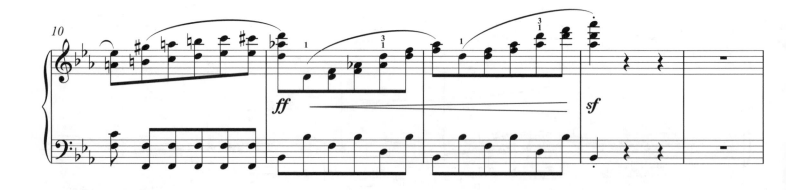

Mazurka in A Minor
Op.17, No.4

Music by Frédéric Chopin
Arranged by Jerry Lanning

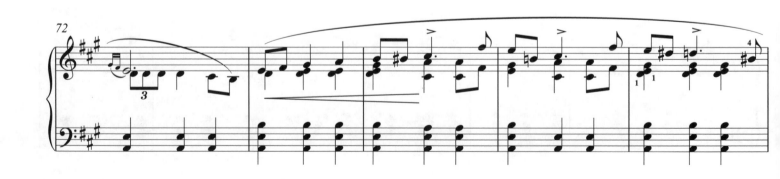

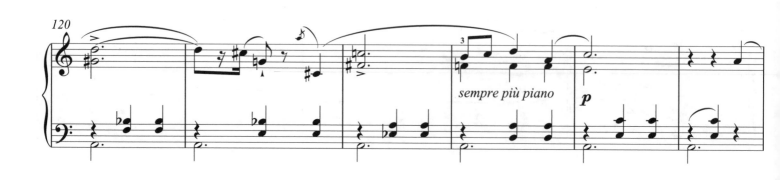

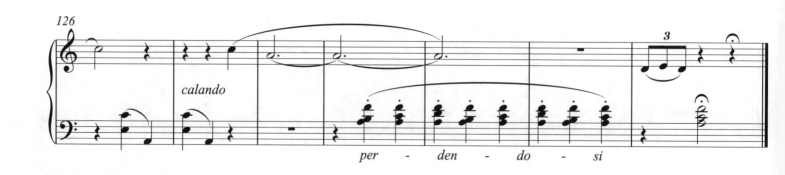

11/06(60252)